Quilt Whispers

Stitched Bonds of Experience, Inquiry, and Growth

DORIS STEINER DIENER

To order additional copies of this book, contact:
Xlibris
1-888-795-4274
www.Xlibris.com
Orders@Xlibris.com

NLT
Scripture quotations marked NLT are taken from the
Holy Bible, New Living Translation, copyright © 1996,
2004, 2007. Used by permission of Tyndale House
Publishers, Inc. Carol Stream, Illinois 60188. All rights
reserved. Website: www.dorisdiener.com

ISBN: 978-1-9845-7855-6 (sc)
ISBN: 978-1-9845-7856-3 (hc)
ISBN: 978-1-9845-7854-9 (e)

Library of Congress Control Number: 2020908469

Print information available on the last page

Rev. date: 05/22/2020

Quilt Whispers

Stitched Bonds of Experience, Inquiry, and Growth

Doris Steiner Diener
Photography by Haley W. Photography
L-D Photos

To my husband, Larry,

whose commitment has forged a path through
the clutter, unfinished projects,
and my unawareness of time;

who has surrounded each of our variety of
homes with natural color and beauty.

Through it all, he continues to love, support,
encourage, and stay committed.

Abundant Thanks

to this amazing team who has helped bring
clarity and connection to the text:

Sheila Atherton, Debbi DiGennaro, and Larry Diener

Endorsements

"An avid quilter and artist, Doris is also a caretaker of the heart and of stories. Her quilts are not merely a hobby—they are expressions of the pieces of her life. As she reflects on patterns and colors, memories and life-lessons, she guides us in considering our own journeys. What messages is the Holy Spirit whispering in our joys and sorrows, successes and failures, our daily rhythms? As one whose default is mindless busyness, Doris' essays encourage slowing down and listening to the voice of the Piece-Gatherer."
Kendra Landis, Homemaker, Writer, Blogger: kendraheatwole.wordpress.com

"Doris' writings show that the multicolored threads of our lives create a design which is determined by the choices we make, the way we live, and the people who touch the soul. She showcases beauty, wisdom and insight with fabric as she challenges us to take a new look at what lies deep within. This is a book you will continue to come back to read over and over to stir your soul."
Rebecca Sommers, Fabric Artist, Teacher, Presenter, Author, Former President of Friendship Knot Quilters Guild, and Mennonite Women USA

Reflective worship. Intricate beauty. These are just a few impressions of Doris Diener's *Quilt Whispers*. Doris walks us through the inspiration behind quilting masterpieces that she has created over the years of her life as a mother and wife. Personal and bluntly vulnerable, her stories intimate our own thoughts about the value of people and the wonder of God's work that we touch daily. This is a book to be read in bits and digested in solitude. Questions at the end of each entry challenge us to seek greater understanding of our lives and our Lord. If handled with the care it deserves, *Quilt Whispers* could well be a life-changing read.
Diane Omondi, Sister-in-Law, Professor, Author, Church Planter in Africa

As Doris Diener shares her rich ancestry of artistry and design with the reader, she inspires a new awareness of the gifts God has placed within us, energizing us to express our own creativity in more imaginative ways. She refreshes us with word pictures and the originality of her quilt creations. She gives tribute to the beauty that emerges as we discover the differences among us, and to all women, including my mother and grandmother, who with needle and thread, repurposed fabric scraps to create quilts for our family.
Ruthann Nyce, Professional Crafter and Seamstress

This book inspired me to sit down at the "sewing machine" of my own craft, and get back to work.
Debbi DiGennaro, MSW, Author, Professor

Contents

Foreword

What is a quilt? This can be answered in a myriad of ways. For some, it is a way to stay warm. For others, it is a tattered keepsake from someone who shared the same blood. And for more, it is simply a way to decorate a home. But if we take a deeper look into a quilt, we see it possesses more than any of these things.

A quilt is a silent partner.

Shortly after our two children passed, I began a patchwork quilt using my stash of fabrics. We didn't have much money as I was taking time off from work to grieve our great loss. We had just moved to a new area of the country, and the now meaningless medical bills began arriving. I poured my tears, my prayers, and my frustrations into that quilt. I named it "The Grieving Quilt." No other person was there while I was creating. The room held me, the fabrics, threads, and (I realized years later) God. That quilt absorbed fallen tears. That quilt absorbed heartbreak. That quilt absorbed anger. It didn't need to speak any words, but it was my silent partner allowing me to feel emotions or be numb, depending on the day.

A quilt is a communal gatherer.

In days past, women would gather together to work on a wedding quilt for a new couple in the community. Words would be shared, laughter could be heard, and sometimes silence would be summoned. Currently, our days are filled with noise and chaos. Families run from one event to another, unable to get there fast enough. Food has become packaged to take on the run. Self-checkout lines are present so that you can set the pace rather than rely on someone else's timing. Mercifully, there are still a few quilting bees in existence. Quilt guilds continue to meet. Women pile into a car to travel to a quilt shop and enjoy a lunch together after purchasing fabrics for new projects. These moments of fellowship occur due to a quilt bringing people together.

A quilt is purposeful.

Each year I reintroduce our Christmas quilts to our home the day after our bellies are filled with turkey. My son gets excited when he notices them on the sofa because this is an unequivocal signal that Christmas day is rapidly approaching. These quilts are purposeful in their sense of timing.

When we are ill, few entities are as comforting as a parent's snuggle or a heavy quilt warming our bones. These quilts share a purpose of contentment, safety, and comfort.

Some quilts symbolize strength and freedom with their red, white, and blue tones. Others suggest reminders of an adventure one had years prior. Still, others are whimsical and command smiles from those around them. Yes, every quilt does have a purpose.

Quilts are storytellers.

When I was primitive in my quilting career, I made a simple quilt but chose to use quilt shop fabrics, something to which I did not feel I could treat myself until I was more experienced, but I was so excited to use those fabrics. The quilt was loved throughout the years. I used it when I took my two young nieces on a picnic in a park. After eating our sandwiches and chatting, I brought out three empty canvases and an array of acrylic paints. The quilt on which we sat was on the receiving end of blue, purple, and yellow streaks of paint that never came off. I now use that quilt to line the trunk of my car, and every time I see it, my heart is full. That quilt told a story of humility, a bit of extravagance, and communion with my nieces. Quilts can chronicle parts of our lives. Much of the time, however, these stories are never told and are folded up and put away with the quilt.

In this narrative, Doris invites us into her past, sharing stories about a life centered around community, family, routine, and hard work, all the while keeping the Lord and Savior the center of her focus. She shares stories of gains and losses. She opens her heart to us, disclosing deep wounds. Doris is raw in her recollections of her past and reveals motives for creating specific elements to her treasured heirloom quilts. What is a quilt? Let us commune with Doris in what she sees in her quilts—whispers of Love, Lord, and Life.

Selena Krajewski, Ph.D. Molecular and Cellular Pharmacology, Quilt Artist, Teacher
February 6, 2020

Introduction: The Piece-Gatherer

What a chaotic mess! The world is full of pieces—pieces of projects, ideas, dreams, and, most sadly of all, pieces of broken people. Some pieces are carried by the winds of time and tornadoes; some litter the landscape, seascape, and cyberspace; some build and some bring disorder; some challenge thoughts, plans, piety, and peace. Pieces of beautiful and broken people surround us, influence us, and indwell us.

But wait! On the distant horizon, the Piece-Gatherer carefully gathers one piece at a time and thoughtfully begins a creative process. Even as he works, he finds the exact place where each piece fits and can contribute to a larger work of artistry. The profit-driven community, with its taunting cynicism, disregards his work as a waste of time and relevancy, for it believes that pieces, regardless of their potential, are to be thrown away. "It is better to start with selected new ones," it says, "because they require less time and resourcefulness."

Shifting our vista, we notice a used and broken form exerting painful effort to rescue the few remaining pieces of what used to be. Somewhere from the mist of the past, she recalls an image of the Piece-Gatherer. Might there be a remote chance for this fragmented nonentity to be rescued from this mess? Is there any hope for restoration and value? With delusions of defeat, the most accessible option seems to be to succumb to the hopeless abyss of worthless, discarded pieces.

Perhaps you and I, with beauty and brokenness, our ideas and dreams, have been torn and our pieces scattered. Perhaps we long to be found by the Piece-Gatherer, revived, transformed, and given a place of belonging. Being a hodgepodge of strength and frailty, inspiration and apathy, I know how it feels to be a collection of pieces that appear to not fit. I have experienced the pain of being torn by the discord of the abstract and concrete, the random and sequenced, the introvert and extrovert, the imaginative and practical, the valued and unvalidated, the delightful and disgusting, the intellectual and ignorant, the insufficient and excessive.

Ah, yes! They all have left their marks, but among the dispersion of the pieces, I have found that I am not alone; there are many of us with similar stories. When our pieces are joined together with the Piece-Gatherer's artistry, we become beautiful.

Listening to the messages of the whispers stitched into my quilt-making processes reveals the spectrum of the conversations between my reality, my heart, and my dreams. Even as I continue to listen, restoration continues.

THE WHISPER OF WELCOMING INVITATION

Quilt: Invitation to Creation
Pattern Background: Tims, Ricky, *Convergence Quilts: Mysterious, Magical, Easy, and Fun.* C&T
  Publishing, Inc., Lafayette, CA, 2003.
Pieced and Hand-quilted by Doris 2007–2017

These fabrics pull me toward a time long ago when the concepts of earth, sea, sky, and light were
being introduced to each other. Converging them together seemed an appropriate method to represent this

dynamic interaction. I imagine the Master Designer delighting in the act of bonding them into a unique space, and his satisfaction with the interdependence of the created components. Because this quilt begged for creation to come forth from it, I appliquéd stems and leaves and added multilayered flowers.

Imagine the twinkle in God's eyes when he said, "Let us make human beings in our image, to be like us. They will reign over the fish in the sea, the birds in the sky, the livestock, all the wild animals on the earth, and the small animals that scurry along the ground" (Genesis 1:26). So God designed humans and invited us to inhabit and care for the earth's miraculously complex exposition of life. The Creator's pleasure and enthusiasm were uncontainable as he anticipated the interaction and continued creativity in all he had made.

There is a profound mystery in the Creator's summons for us to enjoy and care for this lavish exhibition of life, and to thrive as we nurture the flourishing of each other and nature. This incomprehensible invitation needed to be represented in this quilted presentation of creation so I included it with a statement of its source and welcome.

There is a place with our names at the Creator's family table for us to sit and participate in his joy and delight; to learn from this amazing Designer; to bring our diseases and brokenness for compassionate balm and renewed hope from this forgiving Healer. We are warmly invited. How will we RSVP—with willingness or regrets?

Consider with me:

1. In your daily routines, how might an increasing awe of creation's enormity, its detailed and infinitesimal complexity, its fragility and strength, impact your beliefs and choices?
2. How and where do you find your place in this cosmic picture?

WHISPERS OF A SLOWER PACE

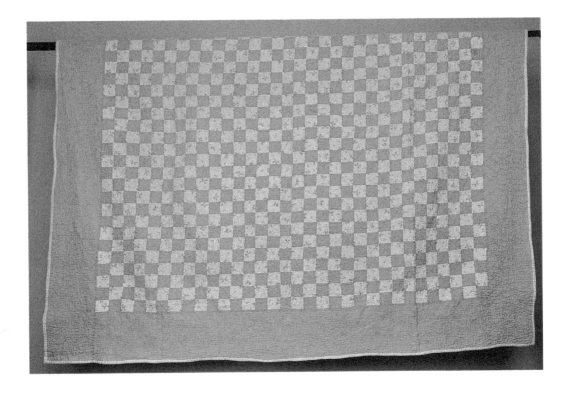

Quilt: Grandma's Quilt
Pieced by Lydia Eberly (1886–1970)
Hand-quilted by Lydia's Family and Friends 1950s

I knew my maternal grandparents well because they lived in a house on the other side of the large garden we shared. In the evenings, Grandma Lydia stitched. She crocheted beautiful articles for home use as she listened to the living room clock and family conversations. In the daytime, she sat at her Singer treadle sewing machine recycling leftover fabrics into quilts. Without any quick cutting or piecing techniques, each piece was cut individually and laid into the desired design on an old sheet on the floor. They were gathered in meticulous order and placed in labeled piles. Then, one by one, they were sequentially sewn into their places.

Grandma wasn't fast, but she was steady and persevering. My mom inherited her "slow" genes and, without giving me a choice, passed them on to me. Once when we three sisters asked which of us was most like her, Mom thought for a while before answering, "Doris is most like me because she's slow, like I am." Thanks, Mom!

In a fast-paced world, a slow pace is outmoded and discredited. Time is equated with money, and money trumps relationships. In truth, I think we all have an inner longing for our lives to slow down, offering us the beautiful gift of feeling and thoughtful processing. A slowed pace reveals unnoticed possibilities that yield irreplaceable rewards. While we all want it, I'm perplexed why we rarely honor those who take time to preserve it.

In my childhood, I don't remember ever purchasing fabric for quilts. We bought fabric to make clothing. The use of these two well-matched fabrics in this quilt poses unanswered questions: Did Grandma confiscate these matching fabrics from the bags of feed that was milled for the animals and delivered to the farm? Did Grandma not like these fabrics? Had she run out of scraps before she had pieced a quilt for each of her thirty-five grandchildren? Had someone gifted them to her?

She was well-acquainted with piecing two-inch blocks because they allowed smaller pieces of leftover fabrics to be recycled. They also easily fit together in simple designs of colorful quilts, which we used to keep us warm in cold weather.

Consider with me:
1. What have we gained from our fast-paced living? What have we lost?
2. How might we honor those who require more time than we think is necessary?
3. In which parts of your life would you value more time?

WHISPERS OF INDIVIDUAL AND COMMUNAL PERSPECTIVES

Quilt: Trip Around the World I
Pieced by Aunt Emma (1911–1996) circa 1960
Hand-quilted by the Leatherman Sisters 2016

In the middle years of the twentieth century, the seasons came and went, each with its offerings and demands. But life was different back then. We worked together to keep the farm flowing and food on the table. In the spring we planted; in the summer we weeded and watered; in the fall we harvested and preserved hundreds of quarts of food for the growing family; in the winter we read, rested, and prepared for the spring.

In spite of the nearby coal communities, no politician needed to convince us of "green." It was the way of life—we saved what we could, we recycled and repaired. We laundered several batches of clothes in the same soapy water. Sometimes the water in the bathtub was passed on to another for a much-needed bath. We prepared the soil with the same tools and well-used equipment. We harvested and preserved our food year after year using the same bowls, baskets, and jars. We sweat gallons in the summer without air-conditioning. We kept warm in the winter under mountains of wools and cottons woven together from the resources of the sheep and cotton scraps from our homemade clothes. The mill that ground the grain for our cattle often delivered it in beautifully patterned cotton feed bags, so we selected the ones we wanted to use for our shirts, dresses, or quilts, returning the others to be reused.

Since Mom did not sew, she had our clothes made by a sister or friend who always returned the unused pieces. She saved them, and at some point, passed them to her sister Emma to sew into quilt tops. These quilts bring back many memories of childhood as we recall specific events where we wore the garments made from the fabrics in their design.

Like much of our lives, work was shared. When quilts needed to be quilted, we invited a group of friends. As a young girl, I played under and around the quilts of women sharing their family events, their feelings of joy and sorrow, fun and dreams, anger and grief, pain and challenges. When I was old enough to help, I often assisted in the preparation and serving of lunch to these quilters, again privy to the conversations that emerged. Then, when I gave evidence of stitches that were even and small enough, I took my place at the quilt.

Yes, teamwork made routine work as enjoyable and light as possible. We played, squabbled, argued, debated, laughed, cried, celebrated, and grieved. We realized our dependency on the weather, the earth, the community, and God as we held our breath in the uncertainties of birth and death, accidents and illness. (My oldest brother Bob, in particular, kept about a dozen guardian angels very busy, protecting him and breathing life into him when his odds indicated that he never should have survived. What an affirmation of extended purpose for him!)

If this is sounding idyllic, it wasn't. Life was real and sometimes very raw. We each tried to find a way to protect the privacy of our inner beings without dishonoring the other, but in truth, we each carry scars of imprinted wounds. Laughter was mixed with blood, sweat, and tears. That is the soil into which I was birthed. And that's how we traveled around our world from day to day, week to week, month to month, and year to year.

Consider with me:

1. What are the advantages and losses of communal experiences? Of autonomy?
2. If you could choose a 40/60 balance of experiences between those done with others and those you do alone, which would you choose to be the greater and lesser? Why?

WHISPERS OF CHANGE AND SPIRITUAL FORMATION

Quilt: Trip Around the World II
Pieced by Aunt Emma (1911–1996) circa 1960
Hand-quilted by the Leatherman Sisters 1916

Aunt Emma took the leftover pieces of our homemade dresses, cut them up into squares, and sewed them into this common pattern, which is truly a testament to the ways procedures and customs change over time. Only God knows all the secrets lost between the stitches of these pieces!

Some of our outfits were sewn from feed bags that were delivered to the farm full of mixed grain for the cattle. Before returning them to the mill for reuse, Dad would pick out the prettiest ones and bring them to Mom. This quilt holds pieces from the remains of those feed-sack dresses of my younger days before the textile business abandoned feedbag-making. Many other squares call forth memories of experiences and their correlating feelings while wearing them—weddings, full skirts to twirl, dates with guys, Sunday best, and broken hearts.

One recurring fabric in this quilt, the textured lavender, is a remnant of an incomplete story. Believer's baptism was an important stepping stone in our spiritual commitment. I had anticipated it for over a year, waiting for my age to arrive at a more acceptable number. When my baptism was finally scheduled, an out-of-state bishop would come to perform this significant expression of my faith journey.

Mom thought I needed a new dress for this special occasion so we went together to several stores to find the perfect fabric. We found it at the local long-gone Spector Store. She had it made into a very simple but attractive dress quite suitable for the occasion.

Well, that's what we *thought*. As the evening of the event approached, the only shadow that hung over me was concern that my knees would crack when standing from the kneeling position. Other than that, I was ready on the inside and the outside.

I don't remember much about that evening other than the bishop's coming to me prior to the service and asking if I had a navy or black dress at home that I could wear. I was confused. Why would *any* girl my age have a dark, somber dress in her wardrobe? It seemed like a very strange question indeed!

The kerfuffle that happened was kept distant enough from me to pass unnoticed until months later when Mom let it slip that the bishop nearly refused to baptize me since I wasn't wearing a dark-colored dress. Even now, years later, I am often curious about what really happened that evening—who was involved in the conversation, how was the conflict handled, and what were the deciding factors of the conclusion!

Mom never indicated any apology or regret for the choice of fabric we had made. The issue was simply laid to rest. That was the way we traveled back then.

Consider with me:
Our belief in a Supreme Being is not forged in a vacuum.
1. What factors have played important roles in your understanding of God and the spiritual realm? How have they changed over time? Why?
2. In what ways might you like to increase your understanding of spiritual intervention in your life?

WHISPERS OF GIFTS FROM THE PAST

Quilt: Bible Verse Quilt
Embroidered by Doris 1960–1995

"I counted. You have fourteen unfinished projects," my husband Larry informed me when he carried in the boxes following one of our family's relocations.

"Ha! Those are just the ones you know about!" I replied.

"Which ones don't I know about?" he asked.

"For one, you have forgotten the Bible verse quilt Mom gave me many years ago."

Throwing up his arms and laughing, he informed me, "You may as well be resigned to the fact that your daughters will need to finish that project long after you are gone!" That challenge was the impetus that carried this embroidery project to its thirty-five-year conclusion.

Throughout my childhood, we lived on a farm where we grew most of our food, ate simply, and lived frugally. We belonged to a large family and were active in our church and school communities. Mom and Dad were happy people who didn't seem to be pressured by the expectations of others. We had what we needed, and I don't remember having many wants.

On one of Mom's periodic visits to a garage sale, she picked up a quilt with embroidered flowers and a Bible verse on each block. I was particularly drawn to that quilt, perhaps because it was a distinct variation from the other bed covers we had.

Most of our quilts were pieced from leftover scraps from our homemade dresses. The quilt "sandwich" was made by layering the pieced top with an old blanket or quilt that needed to be retired, and backing it with a single piece of cotton fabric. It was placed in a large frame to be quilted. Women gathered throughout the next weeks to hand-quilt the layers together with small, even stitches. Those were special times of sharing their lives with each other—supporting, encouraging, and offering advice.

I casually mentioned to Mom that someday I would like to embroider a Bible verse quilt similar to the one she had purchased, never assuming that I would have the opportunity. Then, for one of my early teen birthdays, she surprised me with the extravagant gift of twenty quilt blocks, each marked with flowers and a handwritten Bible verse. This was particularly meaningful because gifts were not common in my childhood and youth. When gifts were given, they were usually things we needed.

My middle and late teen years were filled with many home responsibilities along with church, school, and community activities, so after completing the first couple of blocks, the rest were set aside. When I left for college, the quilt blocks went with me, but my college years passed with few added stitches.

Then I lost the bag of blocks. I looked for them repeatedly throughout the 1970s on my home visits during and after my tenure in Central America, our marriage, and moving all my things from my parental home. They simply could not be found. On a visit to my parents following the birth of our second child in the early 1980s, I decided to do a final search in their unfinished attic for that bag of quilt blocks. Almost invisible in the space between the roof and one of the trusses was a well-hidden box with my name on it. Packaged neatly in their original bag were those twenty blocks. The lost had been found!

Life was filled to the brim with children and family activities, teaching, gardening, studying, and church involvement. A few stitches were added periodically and then the blocks were laid aside again. Now, with Larry's prompting and thirty-five years after their gifting, the blocks were embroidered and ready to be sewn into a quilt. Gathering the family around a display of the blocks on the floor in the order they had been stitched, I gave a commentary about what was happening in my life at the time I had worked on each block.

"I don't want this quilt to cause any trouble between you when I'm gone so this is what I have decided to do: Dad gets to choose his favorite first. Then, each of you teenagers will take turns choosing the ones of your choice. One will be left for me. Dad's and mine will be framed and hung in our home. Each of your six blocks will be made into a wall-hanging for you. So, Dad, you get to choose first."

Silence was rare in our home, but for some time, no one said anything. Then, following some discussion, one of the children spoke up, "No, Mom. These blocks tell a story: They belong together."

"You don't need to worry about me fighting over them!" David announced. "All I want is something pretty that I can hang on my wall and say, 'My mom made that.' That's it. That's all I want. The girls can fight over them if they want, but I won't."

"Are you sure you mean what you are saying?" I asked.

"Yes, I'm sure," he said.

I picked up the blocks in order and placed them back in their original paper bag.

Consider with me:
1. If you could carry some good things from your past into your present and future, what might they be?
2. In moving from one generation to another, what might be intrinsic "things" which may be more important to take with you than visible, physical objects?

WHISPERS OF UNFINISHED PROJECTS

Quilt: In Transit from Past to Future
Embroidered and Hand-quilted by Doris 1996–1999

The workload I was carrying was exhausting, Larry was stressed, and the lives of three active teenagers kept each moment chocked full. My seventy-three-year-old mother, now having relinquished her private independent living apartment to reside with my sister's family on a dairy farm, was increasingly limited to the space between her bedroom and her favorite chair in the living room. She could no longer stand over a sink full of dishes or cook a meal for a table surrounded by guests. As time passed, her frustration settled into a sense of disappointed sadness that gave way to worthlessness. She longed to be a contributor, offering herself in ways that had formerly provided a sense of purpose and value.

One rewarding task she could still do was embroider quilt blocks, which I brought to her. When visiting a craft store, I noticed a package of quilt blocks stamped with a heart. The center of each heart provided a space where a Bible verse could be written. Then I remembered our teenage son's announcement, and it seemed appropriate for me to make him something "pretty that he could hang on his wall and say, 'My mom made that!'" which was similar to what he was seeing when he made his proclamation.

He was coordinated, organized, efficient, and energetic like his dad. He was intense, verbal, and a learner like his mom. Considering our son's nature and gifts, I chose six verses that I thought to be good reminders of his foundation as he sailed the calm and torrential seas of his life. I wrote one in each block, embroidered them, and presented the completed wall-handing. This wall-hanging has hung in *his* family's home in a variety of states and continents.

Those original twenty blocks that had been gifted to me as a young teen and embroidery-completed in my fifties are now stained by the oils from my hands as I embroidered them. They are peacefully resting as an unfinished project, still in that original paper bag in which I received them fifty-eight years ago.

There is a time and a place for about everything so maybe unfinished projects have a purpose too. I know exactly where they are and recall them with a warm, reminiscent smile as I revisit those rich, full days of youth when life was safe and secure, surrounded by belonging and loving acceptance. They pull back a sobering reflection of the years of adventure, responsibilities, as well as disappointment and brokenness. They always bring a twinkle, and they give me a reason to reach into the future and beg for extended time. They patiently, without expectations, wait for me to come up with a pleasing layout as I dream of making it happen—or not—depending. In any case, they provide a trip into the ordinary days of the past. Maybe I'll just allow them to rest and leave them for our daughters to put together . . . or their daughters . . .

Consider with me:
1. How do you deal with the unfinished parts of your experience? Which ones tend to weigh you down? Which ones tend to invigorate you?
2. What feeds or steals the desire within you to live a long life?

WHISPERS OF THE SIGNIFICANCE OF THE ORDINARY

Quilt: Lone Star
Pieced and Hand-quilted by Doris 1984

Lone star quilts, where a single star is the sole focus of the design, have not been particularly drawing to me, but to some, they have appeal. I prefer stars to be in the sky, giving light and providing direction markers. They are part of a larger cosmic community that is constantly present, though often unnoticed. From their distant perspectives, their voices are silent to us, but they share messages of incomprehensible distance, incredible imagination and design, and unfathomable creative strength.

For folks who like this quilt presentation, I offered a series of classes for them to create one of their own. This was the one I made as I modeled the steps along the way. Our neighbor tailored a lovely quilt-hanger for it, and we placed it on the wall of the entrance to our home where it was privy to everyone's comings and goings for many years.

It was there when guests arrived to celebrate all kinds of events—to return our wayward puppy, to participate in meetings, to lend a helping hand or to request one, or to share excitement or discouragement. Women carried their sewing machines past the star as they attended quilt-piecing classes, and students brought their music books to their piano lessons. Instruments and sound equipment were lugged past it in preparation for family performances. It was there when children were taken sick or bleeding to the doctor, when our trusted carpenter came to work on the multiple upgrades on our cabin-esque home, and for the ins and outs of a growing, energetic, involved family. If it could talk, it could tell about all kinds of discussions, debates, arguments, and tears that passed through that entrance. Yes, the star on the entrance wall witnessed it all and much more. It was even there when the burglar broke in on a Sunday morning, and carried out what he wanted.

In the spring, the lone star witnessed the children's going outside to play barefooted in puddles of melted snow, and our eager welcoming of the crocus and tulips as they emerged from beneath their icy snow blanket. We ignored the wall hanging as we prepared the soil for a large garden and nurtured animal babies.

It was there in the summer as we made endless trips to tend the garden, to mow two acres with a push mower, to care for our animals, to go on picnics, and to cut seasoned trees into firewood to provide warmth in cold weather.

It was present through the colorful fall season as we headed back into the school routine, ate ripe apples and apricots, and preserved hundreds of quarts of vegetables and fruits.

Then came the winter's entrances and departures past that star to shovel fresh blankets of snow, to engage in all kinds of snow activities, to enter the artic zone each morning to feed the animals, and remove the ice from the windshields so we could all go to school.

As the first and last thing one saw, the star sacrificed a bit of its luster to all the comings and goings, bluster and fluster of family, friends—everyone and everything—who entered and departed our home. From its position of oversight, it soundlessly gave its greetings and best wishes to all—those who loved us and those who didn't so much—until nearly everything was packed and loaded for our family's relocation to another home in another state.

We may be much like the star—present but uninvolved, observing but not contributing, visible but unnoticed. As we overfill our time and overextend our energy, we may be missing the most important components that are being etched in the lives of those around us. Though present, it is so easy to miss the significance of the ordinary.

Our lives—and those of our children—are built on the consistency of the routine, seemingly inconsequential events and relationships that fill up our days. Nurturing or not, these repetitions form the pathways of our assumptions, beliefs, and values that significantly impact who we are, how we see others, our expectations of those around us, and our concept of God.

Whether we like it or not, we are to be living stars, reflecting God's light and providing direction markers. We are part of a larger cosmic community that is present, even when we are unnoticed. From our perspectives, we share messages that are carried by others into incomprehensible distances, nurturing or dismantling incredible imagination and design, and unfathomable creative strength.

Truthfully, there are times when I would like to be a star on the wall. But I know I could not stay there indefinitely, for I carry the breath of Life, an unmerited gift of mercy and grace that must be passed on to others.

Consider with me:
Obviously, a quilt is an inanimate object making its contribution to the environment. You and I are living beings. Wherever we are, we too help create that environment as we impact others in some way.

As you think of the people whose lives you routinely touch, what kinds of etchings are you imprinting upon/within them?

WHISPERS OF LOST HOPE

Quilt: The Heart of the Cross
Pieced and Hand-quilted by Doris 1998–2017

The distant sky looked ominous as the clouds rolled toward us with intensifying shades of determined devastation. Every front was closing in with foreboding threats: our children were challenged with chronological, geographical, and social adaptations; our promising cutting-edge professions were being undermined, abused, and dismantled; our marriage was internally bleeding. The gradual dismembering of our world into bits and pieces was palpable.

Larry and I were both known throughout the community, and our children were active participants in three different schools. Where does one go for protection, strength, wisdom, and understanding when you live in a glass house? The resources of our inner beings were significantly overdrawn; our friendships lacked longevity and depth; God seemed distant but was the most consistently embracing.

While full of stories of injustice, uncertainty, pain, and defeat, the Holy Bible offers secrets of transforming suffering into blessing. I stitched a few of those secrets in Aida cloth, surrounded them with lace, and placed them under the arms of the cross, to remind me of God's caring presence and His gift of hope.

The cross. Jesus died there. His death was undeserved. He was misunderstood in every dimension. Alone. That's how I felt. He had given his life without guilt, revenge, hostility, or anger to redeem others. Though his reach extended incredibly beyond mine, my inner motivation often propelled me beyond my personal

preferences to embrace the best for others. I was passionate about nurture and care for my family and students, the equipping of the church, respect and dignity for my colleagues, and a vision for the molding and release of all these dear people into meaningful futures. Reflecting on Psalm 30:5, "Weeping may last through the night, but joy comes with the morning," I wondered if my morning would ever come.

Each day I stitched, releasing the pressure of pain as I grasped the application and promise of the verses, but I could not bring myself to sew in the missing piece I always knew was there—a drop of blood falling from his heart. Each time I see this quilt, the drops of blood Jesus shed for my—and others'—wrongdoings are invisibly present.

I tried to decide how to put the blocks together in a way that would preserve the richness of their messages, but at that time, I could find nothing that satisfied. Their background color has long since passed out of vogue and that set of crises has been resolved. About twenty years later when the blocks came together, the truth had more clarity and seasoned relevance than when they were originally stitched.

Consider with me:
With all my heart, I do believe hope exists, though our pathways to find it may be quite different.
1. How do you hold on to hope when circumstances forcefully try to steal it?
2. How might you be submitting to or defending a dissolution of hope?
3. How might you find new hope when the former has dried and blown away?

WHISPERS OF HOPE RESTORED

Quilt: Breath of Wind

Pattern: Variation of "Tumbling Triangles," Pattern by Running with Scissors Quilters. Running with Scissors Quilters & Studio 180 Design, Ltd., 2016.

Pieced by Doris 2019

Machine-quilted by Selena Krajewski

For as much of the year as possible, Larry nurtures his yard to be a lush green carpet. Last fall as the early winds blew, the leaves took their turns tumbling to the ground. He raked them up and bagged the first layer. After each of the subsequent layers blanketed our lawn, the rain weighted and packed them, holding them earthbound. Then the weather turned cold. Hoping for a vibrant crop of spring grass, he and some friends worked to remove the thick layer of frozen leaves to allow fresh air and nutrients into the soil.

Sometimes life gets packed down with layers of stuff that hinder the freedom of fresh vigor. Our ideas gradually lose momentum and hope suffocates. The dark fabric of this quilt represents the weightedness that so often restricts our freedom to offer our best. Rather than submitting to the defeat of tumbling triangles, I saw rising ones. The dark sides seem impenetrable until they are aroused by an invisible breath of wind that jostles their tight hold on each other. The growing spaces between them allow increased movement until, one by one, the triangles are lightened and freed to lift into flight.

As I spent hours sewing the triangles together and working with the layout, my thoughts wandered to areas of my life where I needed a breath of wind to bring new life and perspective. I thought about the Holy Scripture's reference to the invisible wind blowing where it pleases, without our knowing where it comes from or where it will go (John 3:8); wind that motivates action or agitates (James1:6). Wind is an uncontrolled force having potential for good or for ill.

When the winds of our lives offer a new perspective, we risk seeing something that we hadn't noticed before. Seated inside a cozy home and looking at the snow through thick protective windows, we see a soft world draped in gentle white. Handling snow we learn it is wet and cold; shoveling snow reveals that it can be weightless or quite heavy; driving in snow informs us that it can be slippery and hazardous. If our home is not warm or if we have to work all day in blowing snow, our concept of what snow is and how it affects our world changes. Though what we learn from our past informs our present, each new encounter can stretch our horizons. We don't have to be bound by the limitations of our past if we allow the wind to renew our perception.

If the dark colors of this quilt represent inflicted injury, their upward movement as they lighten may represent healing or the forgiveness process. For those of us who find it very difficult to release guilt and forgive ourselves, this wall-hanging can help us with the ongoing task of letting go.

If the dark colors represent a trampled personhood, a breath of fresh identity rustles them into an awakening, nudging them to stir and rise. If they represent unrealistic expectations, a wind of relief or possibility may lift them. If they represent loss, a wind of opportunity may cause a stirring. If they represent discouragement or depression, hope may ride on a whispered breath of wind. As the wind begins to shuffle the layers, the space between them expands. The revitalizing air blows in an increased desire for movement, and bit by bit the layers disperse, ascending into new areas and interactions until, someday, they actually take flight. Rather than triangles cascading downward as the pattern title suggests, I see them rising upward. This design offers hope for an escape from that which we long to release.

This awakening breath of wind reminds me that I can rise again, that the stirring of the mundane can indeed expose possibilities of previously unknown vistas! I can't control the behavior of others, but there is a source of strength that helps me in my daily choices to open my window to delight rather than to despair. I can determine to help rather than hurt. I can choose to overcome irritation with patience. I can opt to forgive rather than condemn. All of us long for authenticity and acceptance, so let's gift them to each other! We each have choices to make, people to influence, and a Creator to represent.

I experience a profound stirring in this quilt that nudges me to feel the wind and release myself to a metamorphosis!

Consider with me:
1. What choices can you make to give space for fresh, rejuvenating air to lift the weights you would like to release?
2. What might be a revitalizing secret that's being whispered to you today?

WHISPERS OF SPROUTING ROOTS

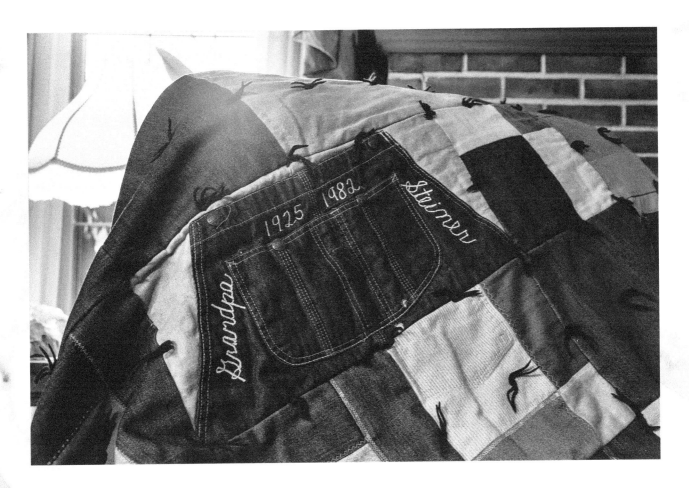

Quilt: Denim Warmth
Pieced and Tied by Doris 1997

Good roots are worth maintaining so they can sprout again in the next season. One attempt to pass on my roots was placing the bib of a pair of overalls my dad, Truman Steiner, often wore, into a warm covering for our son.

The melodies of my childhood had enough rhythm and repetition to wrap it in a sense of purpose and safety but enough freedom for variation and exploration. The experience of growing up on our Ohio farm throughout the 1950s etched much about life into my mind and heart—etchings about beginnings and endings; strengths and weaknesses; joys and sorrows; explainables and inexplainables; good and not-so-good work ethics; sowing and harvesting; dependency on others; dealing with uncontrollable circumstances; problem-solving and compromise; birth and death, et cetera.

Mom taught me the tasks of homemaking, childcare, and gardening, along with harvesting and preserving. She taught me how to laugh and sing even when I didn't feel like it. She lived a life of gratitude, always aware of those who had less. She taught the value of people over tasks and objects. She taught me how to deal with little and with more. There were silent, unseen lines in the sand that we didn't question and she didn't defend, but we all knew they existed and what the expectations were. Mom taught me to enjoy life and have a sense of humor.

There was a special connection between Dad and me. He was a craftsman, an inventor, and a problem solver. As a lifelong learner and a friend, he taught me to think. He taught me that when there seem to be no more options, it isn't because there aren't any but because we haven't thought of them yet. He taught me to walk through the walls of restrictive boxes and to allow others to do the same. He saw and accepted people and could enjoy their mannerisms and uniqueness without being critical or demeaning. His daily attire included a smile with a hint of mischief while the rest of his body was clothed in a pair of sturdy blue denim overalls.

I loved doing farm work—driving the many miles around and around the wheat, barley, oat, corn, and alfalfa fields; raking and baling hay; and pulling grain wagons. I stacked bales on the wagon and in the haymow and helped periodically with the animals.

Dad and I worked well together, father and daughter. Farm work was a part of life for sons and daughters as we each became old enough to help in some way. When we had opportunities for conversation, I asked questions to which he responded, sometimes with answers and sometimes with challenges. I enjoyed thinking with him and probing how he thought and why. Still in his dirty overalls, if he had any discretionary time, it was spent reading the encyclopedias and studying other sources of information.

Consider with me:
1. In what ways have your biological and environmental engravings contributed to who you are today?
2. How are you being intentional about breaking negative cycles that may be a part of your past?
3. What evidence do you see of your roots sprouting in the lives of those you influence?

WHISPERS OF THE PASSAGE OF TIME

Quilt: Denim Warmth (continued)
Pieced and Tied by Doris 1997

Larry and I have a son David who, from the day of his birth, observed with intensity, explored everything, and was powerfully active as he aggressively pursued his goals. His eyes shone with adventure and inquiry as he asked a bajillion probing questions and studied not only to know but also to understand and conquer. He was a boundary pusher, not confined to the ordinary or status quo. Though he was hardly three when my dad passed away, Dad must have felt the surge of common blood between them for, in the short times they spent together, there seemed to be an unusual bond surrounding Grandpa and Grandson. You could see pride and pleasure between them in the way they interacted.

David started walking—no, running—at his Grandpa and Grandma Steiner's home in Ohio when he was eight months old. Back in our Michigan community, if I diverted my watchful eye to hang up laundry on the clothesline, I may find him knocking on the neighbor's door. It was following the service at church where I experienced the most frustration. Wrenching himself out of my arms and maneuvering his hand from my grip, he would run around and between crowded legs in his beeline to an exit. That didn't work so well for me as I frantically trailed behind, pushing my way through the crowd, desperate that my child would be trampled by an unsuspecting friend inside the church or driven down by a moving vehicle in the parking lot.

We read a library of books. One precious memory is reading Madeleine L'Engle's *A Wrinkle in Time* to three preschoolers, two on my lap and one right beside me to catch each word. By age eight, David had exhausted my knowledge of electronics, so I suggested that rather than making small unrelated projects, he undertake a larger endeavor such as the acquisition of a ham radio license. Larry learned Morse code with him and they "ditted" and "dahed" letters and messages until David's speed was up to passing his tests. Within the year, he had his license and was connecting with other ham operators around the world.

His school years were full of articulate conversations and explanations, pet parades, bike jumps, bargaining and persuading, tree houses, skiing, consequences, logic and debates, Bible quizzing, sports, awards and honors, and so much more. In spite of his demand for precision and truth, he was a likeable, fun guy with at least one poignant and well-placed joke for every situation. He was full of passion, ideas, and questions. At nighttime when this verbal processor lay in bed, a caring, feeling child emerged as he reflected on the events of the day—a child of depth, pain, insight, and compassion.

We held on tightly to God's intervening mercy to get him to finish high school. His friends had already graduated, and he begged to spend his school days at the library, arguing that he'd learn more in a day at the library than at school for a week. How might a set of parents who were both teachers explain that?

As the time approached for our David to go to college, a deep sense of grief started growing within me. It was a time of celebrating a significant milestone—one that he thought he was ready for, and I wasn't sure I was. Yes, it was time for my husband and me to release him, and we questioned if we had adequately prepared him for the unknown bumps ahead.

A keen sense of departure and a need to somehow tie the past, present, and future together hovered over me. I decided to make a blanket to keep him warm in the cold weather. As his farewell loomed before me, the memory of my dad's passing seemed to extend its connecting shadow over the anticipation of David's leaving home. Each departed to enter an unknown world, and I knew very well that the past never returns.

Pulling out a pair of my dad's overalls, I decided to make a denim blanket from it and the best remains of David's old jeans. The bib of Dad's overalls is centered at the top with his name and dates. The transfer to David is stitched into the bottom right.

Each time I think of this warm denim blanket, the same sentiments stroke the strings of my heart that I experienced with Dad's death, our son's leaving home, and the uncertainty of the future—each packaged in the passage of time. Now, years later, this same blanket warms his son, our grandson, my dad's great-grandson.

Consider with me:
Time has its way of marching on, regardless of the circumstances of our lives. Sometimes it ushers us into better or worse days, but we can count on change.

1. What are some good people or events that Time has removed from the screen of your life? How have you processed those losses?
2. What are some positive changes that Time has introduced to your experience?
3. Though the past cannot be undone, how might you live your todays to create better tomorrows?

WHISPERS OF DARING TO DISCOVER

Quilt: Debbi's Nine-Patch
Pieced and Hand-quilted by Debbi Diener 1999

There's a special place in my heart for princesses who don't realize their royalty. Debbi, our older daughter, made her entrance into a world that threatened her survival. From birth, she was loaded with allergies that impaired her breathing and digestion. We fought for her life for her first nine months. There is a price required to overcome the odds, and there are also significant rewards.

Debbi prefers to learn by discovery and then, forging forward, adds her own spin, whether it is an unprecedented combination of spices, a collection of wildflowers, spinning new songs and stories, or chiseling wood carvings and relational empires. You wouldn't believe the confusion of savory and sweet spices that flavored some of her early culinary creations! Remember, those were the days before hot pepper and chocolate were combined. (Who knows? Maybe that was a spin-off of her experimentations!) The payoff was that she emerged as a great cook with a palate for food and flavors from all corners of the world.

She had a knack for bonding with her pony, her cat, and difficult people. She continues to have a disarming way of penetrating the heart of a difficult boss, an irate neighbor, a challenging conflict, and a hostile cultural environment. Her unassuming demeanor (although often perceptive, discerning, and strategic) and spontaneous giggle are disarming and invite ease and delight.

When it was time to design her going-to-college quilt, Debbi didn't want one that I made; she wanted to design her own nine-patch collection, choose the fabrics, sew and quilt it, and found delight in doing so. As the years passed, it has traveled with her across experiential mountains of influential successes and through torrential valleys of failure, from one culture and into the next. It continues to hang together as she humbly but confidently passes vision and common sense wherever she happens to be to whomever will receive it.

She's not limited by others' expectations or preferences. She's a messy, losing little love on cleaning, but she's not alone in that. Her appearance is what you see and that's OK, for that is who she is. She deals with complex issues with simplicity and common sense. Though a capable leader, miracles blossom as she casually weaves her presence through the experiences of others as a friend. She tactfully encourages, suggests, and then moves on to another, allowing each person to discover in his/her time and way the truth nuggets she has planted unawares. She perceives, processes, and experiments, teaching and guiding those whose lives intertwine with hers. Debbi moves mountains without anyone knowing quite how she does it.

Among her discoveries, she knows who she is, her sources of enjoyment, and her capabilities. Debbi knows when to step back to free others to perform. She knows that opportunities for discovery are limitless, not dictated by time or location, tradition or fad, or the opinions of others. And if you want to learn to know her, she won't give you a portrait; she will leave that for you to discover.

Debbi has no idea where her quilt is. She thinks that it may have been used for a rag for an auto mechanic. When I asked about finding it for the photo collection, she said:

"I would love to find it, but I also understand that losing stuff is part of an active, dynamic life. My life is about more than cataloging all my treasures in a museum of myself. Sometimes we love our treasures and use them up. In this case, the quilt in question served us in our happy cabin tucked into the folds of the Virginia mountains. If it is lost, it is lost because it was being used and appreciated there instead of stored in a shed somewhere while we were in Africa. And I still have some of the leftover blocks here in my new house" (phone conversation, December 4, 2019).

Her quilt fits into the story as many things fit into our lives. Their significance is in the experience and then we move on.

Consider with me:

1. What are some discoveries you have made? How have they affected you?
2. When have you or others placed expectations on you that have been helpful and when have they hindered your discovery process?
3. How do you respond to Debbi's attitude about using our treasures?

WHISPERS OF SIMPLICITY

Quilt: Elli's Nine-Patch
Pieced by Doris
Hand-quilted by a Friend 2001

Elli, our third child, draws her strength from a source that extends beyond the rationality of a culture limited to its understanding and speculative theories. She was born that way—perceiving more than she knew or could understand. It seems that intuitive people perceive things without knowing the hows, whys, and what-fors. Though we may benefit by considering their unexplainable insight, it is often overridden by those who can articulate reason and provide concrete evidence. Convincing arguments often confuse or dismantle even the strongest sense of discernment.

When I asked her what kind of quilt she wanted to take with her to college, she replied, "I want a nine-patch."

"A simple nine-patch? In rows?" I asked.

If I had really understood this daughter, I might have guessed she would want something simple, organized, and predictable because those qualities help provide definitions and boundaries for her perceptions and feelings. How had I missed it? She would have little desire to complicate the beauty of the simple.

We live in a world of complexity. Sometimes we protect complexity at the expense of simplicity. We may minimize simplicity as naïve or intellectually stagnant. Maybe simplicity is comparable to finding intrigue in a single tree rather than trying to analyze the whole forest. Perhaps the in-depth awareness of one tree can better facilitate understanding the miracle of a forest. Certainly, it is appropriate to learn from both the tree and the forest, each in its appropriate time.

The simplicity of children's observations and descriptions teaches us about reality in a way that is lost in the jumbled messes adults prefer to dabble in. In so doing, sometimes we compromise time and brain space, failing to delight in our children's honest transparency. Instead, we may dull it by heaping upon them complex expectations they are not prepared to manage and should never have to own. Elli's call to the simplicity of her nine-patch quilt offers hospitable welcome to freedom and enjoyment of facing our world in a way that honors the obvious, the real, the unmanipulated, the pure, the simple.

Elli captures the essence of this Native American proverb: "Walk tall as the trees, live strong as the mountains, be gentle as the spring winds, keep the warmth of the summer sun in your heart and the Great Spirit will always be with you."

Elli has now taken flight from home to enter a bigger, complex world. As a professional flautist, her sensitive spirit expresses itself in the life she breathes into the music she performs. From a distance, we cheer for this gentle, caring woman as she faces the challenges which threaten to undo her, never realizing the impact of the beautiful sparkles she scatters around her each day.

Consider with me:

1. What factors help to define and create boundaries for you as you find your way through the messes you have to manage?

2. How do you wish for people to know you—as an individual tree or as part of the forest? Why is this important?

WHISPERS OF SPONTANEITY

Quilt: Bird Quilt
Embroidered by Eva Steiner (1927–2004)
Pieced by Doris
Hand-quilted by Marj Heatwole and Friends 2008

Everything in this world has a beginning and an end. Between the two, there is change. When my younger sister, Grace, and I came upon the blocks for this quilt, we were thrilled because it had become increasingly difficult to find patterns that our mother could stitch as her eyesight became poorer. She had always liked birds, so we hoped these blocks would be able to hold her interest for another several months. Since she could only sew the Xs, I embroidered all the beaks and feet before giving them to her so she wouldn't be frustrated by her inability to complete each block.

When I took them to her, she was living with my sister Marj.

"Dori, Mom is complaining about working with the same colors as she embroiders a set of twelve blocks."

"Oh, that's no problem. You have lots of leftover embroidery floss from former projects, right?"

"Oh, yes," she answered.

"Pull out all the brightly colored floss you have and she can embroider each bird a different color."

The color option threw a curveball to my sister Marj. "Dori, what are you going to do with all these different-colored birds?"

I shrugged. "I have no clue."

Well, all our good intentions didn't turn out quite as we three sisters had planned, but Mom finished them. Marj made sure that those colorful birds were given to me.

I always lay out a set of finished blocks on my bed and look at them for a while to figure out where I should take the project next. When I laid out this set, the birds were lost in a sea of too much white. I pulled out matching scraps for each bird and a leftover green fabric to applique, each on two sides of the blocks.

After these colors were added to each block, the second layout begged for more color that would bond the blocks into a more cohesive unit. I added a Hawaiian floral fabric to each corner.

Then came the third assessment. It needed to be larger so I added borders, allowing it to fit our queen-sized bed. After black had made its outlining definition, a white border seemed to be the best option because it would tie the inside of the quilt with the outside. But plain, untextured white lacks interest so I added some random green lines which morphed into "vines." Vines have to have leaves.

The lonely vines and leaves begged for colorful 3D flowers to bloom on them. Gathering lids of varying sizes from the kitchen to use for patterns, I cut circles and made many flamboyant yo-yos, some to use as single blooms, while others were doubled or tripled. Visiting my button box, I completed each blossom with a button in the center. There were no duplicate flowers.

The next evaluation dictated the concluding statement of a pieced border of eight-inch richly colored blocks of many patterns.

This quilt makes a colorful proclamation but other than that, it is not particularly spectacular—it just happened as one unplanned stage merged into the next. During its spontaneous growth, something was happening. There was dynamic, new delight in each development that obliterated any tedium, any obligation to a pattern or expectation of the finished product.

Goals give ideas direction. Plans provide definition. Strategy offers a plan of action. We can build a strong case for all of these. But that's not the way this quilt found its expression. Some of my quilt projects have been carefully charted in advance.

Throughout our days, weeks, months, and years, there are times when objectives and strategies facilitate our reach for goals. This quilt, however, simply emerged, one unplanned phase after another. And that kind of spontaneity, too, is part of life. Not everything can or should be charted. In this case, my impromptu decisions turned into a unique presentation of color and delight.

Each of us has something to offer. We may not consider either our presentation or our offering as being very consequential in the scope of things, but the process over time is profoundly important and perhaps what contributes most to our value. Someone somewhere invested significantly in the provision of our potential and resources. I have a feeling that our Creator finds deep joy and unbridled delight when we choose to let him craft us according to his—and our—pleasure.

Consider with me:
Hindsight is always clearer, but we make decisions in real time.
1. What are some good choices you have made? Which choices could have been better?
2. What kind of investments might you be making into the lives of others and what risks are you taking?

WHISPERS OF CHALLENGE

Quilt: Caleb's Quilt
Pattern Idea: Smith, Louisa L., *Strips 'n Curves: A New Spin on Strip Piecing*. C&T
    Publishing, Lafayette, 2001.
Pieced and Hand-quilted by Doris 2006

The circle of life has predictable seasons and patterns, but most of our daily lives do not follow a script. However, there is security in the familiar. We feel safe when we use the same well-worn paths. Maybe they are easier, simply requiring less time, attentiveness, and ingenuity. Our nature tends to hold on to that which we know—that which is predictable. But we all have times when the pavement of life demands a detour from the straight and symmetrical, and we must consider other ways to reach our destination. A palette of options may take us in different directions or cause unanticipated responses.

Sometimes I am conflicted by my internal irregularities. There's enough pragmatism in me to find little joy in recreating the wheel: If I am very happy with the taste of the food I have prepared, I will try to replicate it another time (even though I seldom use recipes). There's enough adventure in me to lose enthusiasm with repetition: I love to find new ways to locations I frequent. There's enough risk to be intrigued by exploration and discovery: How did the snake ever molt this perfect skin? There is delight in creating something I've not seen before.

Louisa Smith offered a welcomed escape from routine squares and triangles at about the same time our first grandchild, Caleb, arrived, exposing a new era and a more distant horizon, just like the idea of combining strips with circles in my quiltmaking.

This piecing technique lures me much like it did when I made Caleb's wall hanging, because the options it exposes continue to intrigue me just as Caleb's shores continue to stretch my vista. Watching him build his fleet to take him wherever he is going never ceases to amaze my aging mind. His passion to learn burns brightly, and his expectations of what he may be able to accomplish with that knowledge are specific and larger than life as he challenges himself and those around him. While his charm and knowledge draw people to him, his intensity can spawn discomfort. Standing on the shore, I feel pride and concern as I watch with wonder and awe as he enters seas I hardly knew existed.

I didn't have art lessons to teach balance and perspective, but Louisa Smith was there to guide me in my venture with strips and curves. Caleb didn't come with an instruction manual or maps to his specific destination, but there is a guidebook of how God has worked with his people throughout history that may offer some clues.

Louisa Smith invites me to entertain some new ideas. She gives me guidelines for a technique that allows for experimentation and adventure beyond the familiar paths. She encourages me to find my own expression of her technique. I had so much fun with the play-creation of Caleb's wall hanging! (It even includes leftover fabric from an outfit I made for his dad when he was eight months old.) Caleb gives me the same invitation to experiment, to participate in fun adventures, and to forge new paths. Of course, this includes risk, messiness, frustration, trial and error. That's the nature of sculpting something heretofore unknown.

Sometimes his perspective seems a bit distorted and its balance, disquieting. I can relate with curves where it seems straight lines should be and straight lines where curves would be preferable, where textures and colors seem a bit out of sync, when the mile markers and time allotments don't jive, and where the appearance seems unreasonable. But I am very confident that the fragments will come together for him, creating something of lingering value and craftsmanship, just as the crafting of his wall hanging came together for me. I'm also inclined to think that it won't be limited to straight lines. What an honor it is to be part of his life and I hope he senses my affectionate support even though distance separates us.

On a much less significant level, that's what happens in putting together pieces in new ways to create new designs when I weary of the forged paths. Caleb's wall hanging, a fun and imperfect-like-me creation, provided a delightful adventure—like a canoe trip that includes some unanticipated currents.

Consider with me:

1. How do you respond to new ideas? How do you respond to people who nudge you toward them?
2. How do you manage the differences between people who are trailblazers, managers, and workers? In which category are you most comfortable? The world desperately needs all of us!

Quilt: A Solitary Song

Quilt Background Technique from: Tims, Ricky, *Convergence Quilts: Mysterious, Magical, Easy, and Fun.* C&T Publishing, Inc., Lafayette, CA, 2003.

Pieced and Hand-quilted by Doris 2003–2005

Despite the Native American legend that the Sarasota area was a safe haven from angry skies, the trajectories indicated that there was little chance of escape from this hurricane as it churned and turned in the Gulf of Mexico, destined to head back east. We were as prepared as we could be. The house was boarded up, all the garden furniture and movable paraphernalia had been brought inside, and preparations for food and fluid had been made. The roadways north were glutted with evacuees. We had chosen to stay and face the brutal punishment for living in this natural coastline paradise.

The city was blanketed by a toxic tension as it waited for the electricity to go down, roofs to be blown off, and homes to be crumbled. I retreated to my craft room and pulled out a piece of brightly colored "nature" fabric (which, more than a decade prior, had been our younger daughter's skirt) and a few matching fabrics from my stash. In this inner sanctum, the delight of creation took precedence over concern for the destruction which threatened it.

The hours passed as I cut and stitched following Ricky Tim's excellent guidelines. The electricity and our home remained stable as the hurricane entered Florida's mainland through the mouth of the Peace River, lashing its fury on dear ones south of us.

As the storm signaled its passing, I stood back to evaluate my work. My attention was drawn to the bird in the bottom left corner. It was the only one in this fabric jungle who stood upright and complete to face its world. Then, I "heard" a simple, solitary melody emerge from this little creature, offering its world an alternative perspective. Sometimes, even in the midst of life's chaos, we may be surprised by a sudden, unexpected invitation to awareness; an invitation that, against all odds, penetrates the spinning frenzy and lands, silently, in the soul.

Regardless of how contrasting our circumstances may be, we each live in an environment where a variety of symbolic storms occur, stripping us of power, redirecting our choices, and leaving a trail of devastation. The ideas and feelings we feed do grow within us, so at some point, we choose the "melody"—the invitation to awareness—allowing it to permeate our thoughts, feelings, and actions. The supply of hopes and dreams

is not exhaustible, but sometimes it needs to be adjusted as the storms come and go and the seasons of our lives change.

The metallic gold quilting stitches on this wall hanging emerge from this single bird. Their swirls fill the space with the bird's song like a mist of consciousness and awe that brings nourishment to what lies deep within.

Maybe someday, you and I may be like this bird, offering our message of affirmation, encouragement, hope, or healing that reaches into the hearts of those who are listening.

Consider with me:

1. A Chinese proverb in my fortune cookie yesterday that others have quoted is, "Fear is the darkroom where negatives are developed." How do you respond to that saying? Why?
2. Storms threaten each of us. When you must face fear and anxiety head-on, how do you, without denial, disempower their negative strategies that pilfer your strength and joy?
3. What might you have to offer a world that is whirling in the devastation of lost hope and dreams?

Quilt: Father's Quilt
Pieced and Hand-quilted by Doris 2015

My father-in-law, Edward Diener (1917–2016), was a pastor throughout his forty-five-year career. He enjoyed studying the Scriptures and keeping up with the worldwide church. He loved interacting with people and could establish camaraderie and ease with anyone. He was an excellent teacher and preacher, as well as a peacemaking servant-leader.

We added an apartment for him and my mother-in-law to live with us. They moved in when he was ninety-one. He was a dedicated caregiver for his wife, who passed away within the next year. This increased his time to study and offer pastoral visits to other senior citizens.

Father lived with us throughout most of his nineties, leaving this world on October 16, 2016, just before turning ninety-nine. He was a good man and a good friend who died loved and lonely.

People of faith are imperfect, regardless of their role or position. A new pastor came to town with goals of recreating the church's appeal and constituency, which required a redirection of an already active working force. His original intentions may have been well-meaning, but they left a trail of wounded parishioners. Father was one of the innocent victims.

Father was so content in his apartment. He knew many people and enjoyed interacting with them in their homes and at community gatherings. When the church leadership no longer had space for our services, we needed to relocate to a new community twenty hours away. Father handled it like a loyal trooper, for he was thoroughly acquainted with the downside of human nature—even among members of pastoral leadership.

The challenge came as his reservoirs of personal value, growth, and sharing became drained by his loss of familiar people, places, and significant mutual friendships. Though his keen mind still had understanding and insights to offer, ninety-six is not a good age to start from scratch to develop new bases of influence or deep relationships.

He and I spent many hours together discussing, debating, and digging into theology with its beliefs and practices, rewards and consequences, historical and future implications. Father was lonely, and Larry and I could not fill the cavernous vacuum that he profoundly felt. Though new acquaintances reached out to him, their lives were not anchored in his past and didn't intersect in the workings of his daily routines. Since there were no familiar handles for him to grasp, he struggled to hold on to the names and details of these new friends.

He worked hard to keep his world as large as possible for as long as possible. He faithfully watched the news and read about world events. After each of my seminary classes, he would want to know about its content. But the walls gradually moved in, squeezing him into a space hardly big enough for one. Then, I lost a friend.

As Father's world became smaller, we wanted him to be reminded that he was loved and was a person of value and purpose. Larry and I tried to encourage him in many ways, including the wall hanging I made for him. As a daily reminder, it hung in a location where he would see it often until he passed away peacefully in our home one autumn afternoon. It says, "I will be your God throughout your lifetime—until your hair is white with age. I made you, and I will care for you. I will carry you along and save you" (Isaiah 46:4).

Consider with me:
1. Probably the most profound lesson Father taught me was to keep my world as large as possible as long as possible. How are you keeping your world big even now in your current season of life?
2. In what ways can you help others to look beyond themselves in their thinking and compassion for others?

WHISPERS OF A CHANGE OF HEART

Quilt: The King's Kats
Pieced and Hand-quilted by Doris 2017

In my long-passed more formative years, animals were animals and people were people, and there was no confusion between them. Animals, for the most part, had their tasks in the outdoors and humans performed theirs in a flow between the inner and outer arenas. It was not an emotional or psychological matter, but a pragmatic one that had clear and simple boundaries.

Admittedly, I like the softness of a long-haired feline, but not on my coat or carpet. Their temperament is unpredictable and highly preferential. Their odor is absolutely unforgivable. This may help explain why I have no affinity for cats. My authority to address this subject is based on my years of experience with outside cats and a few years of sharing the inside of my home with them.

When I lived in Central America, a family was leaving the country and wanted a good home for their two Siamese cats. Out of the bigness of my heart and the smallness of my brain, I accepted their priceless gift. In all fairness, the cats made an unusually smooth transition of loyalty to me and rarely caused any problems. Once, from their sidewalk view, two children were captivated by these unusual animals and came to my screen door to get a better look. (Cats there were rarely domesticated.) All was fine until I walked over to greet the young visitors. They noticed that my eyes were blue—just like those of the cats. Shouting with their faces reflecting fearful panic, they ran for their lives.

Two things called forth a change in this arrangement of peaceful cohabitation. First, a compatriot needed a home. A local pastor asked if Ms. Di could live with me and share the rent. It sounded like a great idea, so she moved in. The second was the unpardonable mistake that I made in not considering the cats' perspective. Ms. Di said that they were always docile when I was home, but the moment I walked out the door, they targeted her for destruction. As it worsened, she thought they stalked her and she started to have dreams about them attacking her jugular. This did not make for a very harmonious living situation.

After she moved out, they continued their amiable demeanor, *but* when I was gone, they became unruly. During my absence, they shredded my homemade drapes and became much more destructive. This simply could not continue—either they moved out or I did. Since I paid the rent, I decided they were the ones to go. I dutifully transported them to another part of the city and deposited them in what I thought would be a friendly environment for them.

Four decades later:

As I was checking out of a fabric store, the owner said, "Oh, and something you did not see is this collection of corresponding bolts of cat fabrics."

"I think I have purchased enough fabric for today," I responded, but I thought to myself, "Cat fabrics? *No thanks*!"

But then . . . my mind transported me many miles to another continent where a precious grandchild was completely infatuated with these creatures. Shad and his family moved to Africa when he was six months old, so our worlds were always distant. Our interactions lacked the spontaneity of familiarity and I longed to be able to be a meaningful part of his reality. My heart melted as I thought of Shad.

"Let me take a look at them," I said. The fabrics were artistically flattering beyond any feline merit that I could in a hundred years imagine, so I bought just enough fabric to make a nice wall hanging for this precious grandson. He'll never realize the sacrificial love I poured into those stitches, but that's OK. After all, that's what grandparents do, isn't it?

Consider with me:
1. When might you have experienced a change of heart? What motivated it?
2. When might your heart's presets hinder better choices?

WHISPERS OF REVITALIZING PEACE

Quilt: Fertile Peace
Pieced and Hand-quilted by Doris 2010

During a time when I was being personally and professionally suffocated and needing fresh air, we decided to build a greenhouse to raise perennial plants to sell. It was intended to counteract our shrinking perspective of our life and purpose. It was our attempt to move beyond walls dictated by others' expectations and restricting perceptions. It was our attempt to reach beyond the smothering forms of empty legalistic traditions that maintained conformity to a hierarchal system which understood the value of money more than of nurturing and releasing people to pursue truth and character. We turned to nature for a wholesome restoration of equilibrium and growth.

We read and talked with other greenhouse owners and operators, acquainted ourselves with the relevant legalities, and worked very hard to make it successful. It was!

One of the most captivating memories that continues to resurface is stepping from the cold world of January's icy gray and snow into the fertile green of thousands of baby plants eager to become what they were intended to be. The fragrance of oxygen-rich air still invites a momentary pause for a deep, invigorating breath. After stepping inside the greenhouse, I would often fasten the door behind me and stand, eyes closed, allowing the full palette of senses to fill me to overflowing with life-giving peace.

Several years later when we needed to make a decision to expand our little business or let it go, Larry and I decided that our passion was more to nurture people than plants. The greenhouse had fulfilled its purpose, so we sold it. Besides being a great learning experience, it became a symbol of resilience and restoration in a time that could have significantly impaired us personally, professionally, and spiritually.

Years later:

The planned trip to meet our daughters in Europe and then return by way of Africa with our daughter Debbi was now less than two months away. I had nearly forgotten that she wanted to have a wall hanging for the guest house in her expanding East African city. After nixing the options of buying a finished wall hanging from the local quilt shop or the church's sewing circle, a visit to my fabric stash opened the door of possibilities. Finding some fabrics with an African flair, I set to work on this simple pattern. The only consistency was the small black square in a corner.

It was so much fun! Some of the large squares begged to be put together in differing ways. One by one, the stack of pieced blocks magically grew until, at some point, I realized I had way too many! Separating the warmer colors from the cooler ones produced enough blocks to make two wall hangings. The warmer combination I entitled "African Passion," for it evoked a feeling of affection that called me back to my own years outside the USA in the faraway tropics. That was the quilt that found its home in the guesthouse in East Africa.

Each time I sat down to work on the cooler assortment of blues and greens, the greenhouse-in-January memory returned, ushering me into a world vibrant with fresh oxygen and ripples of pregnant peace waiting to release their healing balm and spread the joy of Life set free. There was no better name for the whispers of this quilt than "Fertile Peace."

After finding a balanced layout, I contemplated for weeks on how to quilt it. How could I capture that ripple effect of peace that moves continuously outward, filling the space within its reach? Peace gently throbs with a desire to be shared. I decided to quilt spirals bumping into other spirals. You probably won't notice them unless you look at the back of the quilt, but *I* know they are there, gently nudging me to throw another peace pebble into the water of my life.

Consider with me:

1. Energy and enthusiasm are often the motivators of action. What motivations are triggered by peacefulness? What impact might it have on your daily routines?
2. How might you create an environment of fertile, revitalizing peace?

WHISPERS OF THE GIFT OF SELF

Quilt: Cathedral Windows
Pieced by Doris circa 2003

"Dori, teach me how to make a cathedral window quilt," invited my sister Marj.

"Sure!" I responded. I didn't have a clue how to do it, but I certainly intended to find out!

One of the most profound benefits of teaching is what one learns in the process of preparation. Another is an open door to facilitate learning for someone else, and what a joyful privilege it is to lead another person through that door! The passion to share what I know that may enhance the life of another, pulses through my veins, offering meaning and fulfillment. Her request was an invitation for me to learn something I didn't know and to have the privilege of passing on that acquisition to her!

Marj learns quickly, especially if she can see the process. Step by step, we walked through it. Once she was well established on her project—which developed into a beautiful queen-sized quilt made from fabric scraps that have their own stories to tell—I opted to make smaller wall hangings. This one in jewel tones is a symbolic portrait of my granddaughter Miriam's ethereal proclivities. Let me tell you about her so you can catch the correlation between the two.

Miriam seems to be an abstract random thinker. When I think about her, I think our world would be wiser to validate and nurture perception beyond the realm of the physical senses. Instead, we tend to curdle sensitivity with intensity and measured expectations. We sometimes wound delicate feelings with demands for an acceptable rationale. Sadly, we are good at destroying the process of bringing together the invisible pieces as well as obliterating the simple joys of *being* by the culture's demand for homage to the ever-ticking clock. The bubble room where Miss Miriam lives is vulnerable to the sharp edges of concreteness, time, and the busyness of productivity.

She loves nature and animals and finds delight in the miracles of growth and change. What happens within her as she intently watches with wonder the wounded butterfly she holds on her hand? She is very articulate. She is a little feather of a ballerina. Some of us are people-bodies with hearts; she is a heart confined by a people-body.

Cathedral windows are symbols that embody so much more than the sum of their parts. They represent all kinds of artistry from glassmaking, to design, to telling stories long past, to creating ambiance, to communicating truth, and to calling forth that which is within us. One of the most fascinating qualities of cathedral windows is the myriad of ways they reflect light. They are a paced kaleidoscope bringing together so many variables to present a fleeting, uncaptured, unrepeated reflection. They, too, are vulnerable—so easily broken.

Maybe Miss Miriam has the capacity to reflect the light in ways the rest of us have no time or space to perceive. Maybe she has a potential for dimension that extends beyond observable facts and measured realities. Her uniqueness often has difficulty fitting into our scheduled days and activities. Maybe she has more to teach us than we, with our impatient practicality, are willing to take time to learn as we juggle the segments of our lives to fast, complex rhythms. Maybe she's not a juggler at all but a light diffuser, spreading out light's intensity to present a gentle warmth that is nurturing and protective to plants and people. Maybe. As the sun shines into our atmosphere, those beautiful windows respond. Maybe Miss Miriam is natured like that. And, though sometimes I am challenged to understand the messages of her heart, from her flows a restful, observant, joy of being.

Consider with me:
1. If you could display your heart on the outside, how might it present you differently than people know you?
2. How can you find and maintain significance in who you are regardless of others' perspectives and expectations?
3. How can you give *the gift of being* to others, especially to those you don't understand?

WHISPERS OF CONFORMITY AND DIVERSITY

Quilt: Commentary on a Square
Embroidered by Eva Steiner (1927–2004)
Pieced by Doris
Hand-quilted by Marj Heatwole and Friends

Humility can be a difficult concept to articulate because it never draws attenti[on to a]
quality that we give much attention to developing because, when we do, it vanishes. [...]
cheaply in the marketplace of human assets. What might a picture of humility look l[ike?]

We had just dropped off our daughter and started home. Soon after making a le[ft onto a]
county road, we met a police car headed in the opposite direction. Larry looked in his [...]
noticed that the car had turned around and was heading toward us. As the car approa[ched, he]
turned on his lights for us to pull over. We wondered what the problem could poss[ibly be. We]
must have a nonfunctioning exterior light.

"Do you know you nearly got me killed just now?" he shouted angrily in the win[dow.]
"No, I wasn't aware of that. It seemed there was a significant distance between us[...]
"You nearly got me killed!" he repeated and continued with his belittling accusati[ons.]
My truth sensor was flashing a deep red as steam rolled out of my pores. What w[...]
When we pulled out, he was a healthy football field away from us. Even if he had bee[n over the]
speed limit, he would have been safe. I was livid!

Larry responded respectfully to his questions. As the officer started to write a tick[et, my anger]
ignited. No audible sounds came from the passenger seat, but the inaudible ones wer[e...]
not so nice. This whole thing was *so* wrong!

Falsely accused without anger or retaliation. Calm in a volatile setting. Stead[y under]
intimidation. Guiltless in blame. This is a picture of strength—a strength that many[...]

Larry is a peacemaker who often chooses nonviolence even when it means bearing[...]
another's guilt. He is respectfully honest and knows that logic doesn't make sense to a[...]
doesn't embellish or lie. He asks a poignant question or makes a well-grounded state[ment and backs]
off. His manner has been mistaken for weakness but repeatedly, his contributions have [...]

He remembers the details of conversations and events with clarity, enabling him to b[...]
programs, and forge highways between individuals and groups. Perhaps, because of his ow[n...]
seems to intuitively sense wounds in others. He patiently accepts them where they are an[d...]
a better place. He is a servant from the inside out. Everywhere he has been, he has left a hi[...]

Larry draws encouragement from the book of Psalms, learns from the examp[le of...]
strengthened by the Spirit within him. As he has watched others receive credit for his i[deas...]
"Much more can be accomplished in this world when it doesn't matter who gets the c[redit." He can]
be "unoffendable"—even when wounded. His desire is to leave places—and people—b[etter]
than before he arrived. His yearning for balance protects him from distorted extremes.[...]
opinions, but not his code of ethics. He doesn't show favoritism or take bribes. He [...]
anchors deep. He asks for very little.

You can see that when Larry brought me a stack of T-shirts and requested that [I make a]
memory quilt, there was no question whether or not I would do it for him. This quil[t...]
his life investments where he touched the lives of others and walked with them to a b[etter place.]

(Note: In my acquaintances, there are law enforcers who are worthy of highest reg[ard. They]
are individuals, just like you and me.)

Consider with me:
1. Who in your experiences have modeled humility? How have you noticed it?
2. Why is genuine humility so rare, so costly?
3. Why might you sometimes mistake confidence for pride and humility for we[akness?]

This quilt exhibits a restful, unimposing simplicity of squares as they collaborate with each other to form an attractive presentation.

Mom embroidered these twelve floral blocks. Wanting to give these beautiful blocks a proper dignity, I added the centers of the flowers to add color. Then the challenge began. Though each square has four equal sides, squares come in all sizes and can be placed in different positions.

As I studied the center medallion, its too-perfect presentation lacked drawing interest. But what did it need?

It is easy for a square to fit with other squares just as it is relatively easy for people to find a comfortable fit alongside those with whom they have much in common. When we are surrounded only by those like us, it is easy to assume that sameness shares a bed with rightness, and thus, take for granted that others think like we do—or at least they should. This collaborating comfort clothes us with confidence, making it so easy to become exclusive and judgmental, justifying superiority and entitlement. We may slip into a pattern of assuming that others will carry responsibilities that are ours to own, forgetting that perhaps we should be offering assistance to those who are less capable. The thought of legitimizing someone of a different "shape" into our "pattern" is not attractive or compelling, regardless what he/she may have to offer.

Considering the leftover fabrics, I noticed I had cut too many circles for the flower centers, so I changed their identity to bubbles and randomly placed them to float among the squares. These daring bubbles left their colony of circles to float in a new world where they would bring delight, challenge, and a touch of adventure. For me, they bring life to this *Commentary on a Square* without diminishing its cohesion, pattern, or beauty.

There is a time for organization, symmetry, and balance, but often the moments of perfect order are quite brief and we find ourselves once again being challenged to recreate a sense of equilibrium. We may be surprised to find it unexpectedly in an unusual place or provided by someone we never would have imagined.

Consider with me:
1. For me, the bubbles relieve this quilt from being just an ordinary quilt and they add interest that may inspire questions. What do you think they add or take away from the whole?
2. What are the advantages and the downsides of conformity?
3. What are the advantages and the downsides of diversity?

Quilt: Larry's Memory Quilt
Pieced by Doris
Machine-quilted by Selena Krajewski 2020

Quilt: Celebration of Completion
Pieced by Marianne and Doris
Hand-quilted by Doris 2018

Occasionally, in the course of a day, without any explanation, we are caught unawares and find ourselves profoundly drawn by something incidental. That was my experience as each quilting stitch on this small piece found a deeper lodging in my soul. Why was this insignificant block affecting me so deeply? Each of the four seasons holds mystery for me, but it wasn't until I had penned the poem that I realized that perhaps I was stitching my hope for the reality of my present.

Each season of life offers a hidden cache of secrets to be sought, discovered, and embraced. Spring exposes a peek into the miracle of new life, inspiring us with the unknowns of what has been stirring all winter. Summer is a time to live into our purpose, challenged only by the warding off of all that may seek to destroy or deter it.

For me, fall captivates intrigue as it releases the responsibilities of the spring and summer, freeing nature to relish its fruitful accomplishments and float with abandon on the cooling winds. Winter is a mystery of death and regeneration. Spring, the harbinger of the seasons, introduces new beginnings and later, winter respectfully lays them to rest and prepares for a new cycle.

Marianne is a gifted crafter, but she was new to quilt-piecing when she entered the class. I gave several options for assembling blocks using squares and rectangles and modeled the techniques. Then, it was time for the class participants to begin the construction of their block of choice, putting to practice what they had just witnessed.

Marianne had this worried look as she said, "Doris, I don't know if I can do this. I'm not sure I want to cut into my fabrics because the block might not turn out."

I went to my drawer and pulled out a simple combination of fabrics for her to use for her trial run. She produced a perfectly constructed creation. With her confidence well-established, she proceeded throughout the classes producing meticulously pieced works.

At the conclusion of the sessions, she gave me her trial block. "These are your fabrics and they don't really match mine. You can have this block if you want it because I don't know what I would do with it."

"Are you *sure*?" I asked.

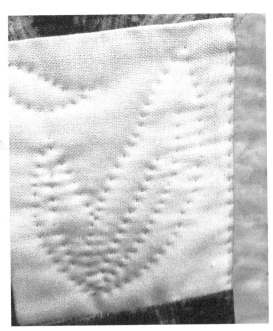

After studying it for a while, I added the gold edge and the border which framed it nicely, but the block still begged for more detail. I added the crocheted doily, leaves, and flower.

How to quilt this block became my nemesis. To break the impasse, I quilted three laps around the appliques. In that process, its message shouted to me, revealing the joyful, simple freedom of the turning leaves as they floated in and out of the printed squares. Making patterns of four differing leaf shapes in the fabric, I traced them onto the plain blocks to be quilted in gold thread.

As I quilted these leaves gliding in the wind, my thoughts were captivated by the freedom of having finished their spring and summer tasks and their release to freely celebrate the completion of their work. I laid aside my needle to pen the following:

Celebration of Completion

There is freedom in completion—
A release when a task is done;
A setting down of a labored journey
As a liberating flight is begun.

The weightlessness of fulfillment
Gives entrance to a reviving breath
That lifts with a joy of abandon
The fear of impending death.

When nature has completed its purpose,
It is time to bid earth adieu,
To allow new life to awaken
A creation that is vibrantly new!

Then, moved to tears, I realized this is where I am in the scheme of my life. Like each leaf at the end of its season, I also want to release my life with a satisfying abandon and celebrate its completion. The three-year-old diagnosis of a terminal illness has brought the brevity of time to fulfill my purpose into clearer focus. It invites an assessment of accomplishment. The awareness of being a part of a process much larger than the sum of its parts dawns with fresh consciousness. I am one of many, but I *am* one. Being uniquely created affirms my significance in the lives of those who have become a part of mine. I have come to see myself as a peasant seed planter, dropping seeds wherever they may fall with the hope that they will someday produce something wonderful and good, right and true. And eternal.

Perhaps this incurable illness has increased the importance of celebrating completions as the need to relinquish meaningful roles and responsibilities reoccurs as my strength drains away. My heart's desire is to complete the tasks for which I was created and then, with peaceful satisfaction, to let go. And celebrate.

Consider with me:

1. What secret might the present season be whispering to you? What should you be celebrating today?
2. What might help you experience peace when your time comes to lay down meaningful parts of your life?

Conclusion

The quilts I have shared narrate portions of my experience and relationships. My choices of design, color, placement, and stitching call me back into my past, reflect on my present, and lure me into the future. My stitches have given voice to my thoughts and feelings, and in some cases, they have provided a wordless answer to probing questions. Some quilts have forged the venue for discovery of a loved one's identity. Some have voiced learning in the sadness of loss, while still others have provided an artistic diversion from fear and stress. Some quilts have given expression to truth under fire, and there are those that have simply been a fountain of joy and delight. This hobby, always packaged between the folds of many commitments, has offered a reprieve from the constancy of expectations and demands. It was—and continues to be—a place where I can experience the peace and enjoyment of being at home with my real self.

My days are full of these stories and many more. In the quilts I've shared, my childhood and adulthood are present, my parents as they aged, our children, and a few of our grandchildren. There are more quilts that haven't been shared, and there are those that are in various stages of the creative process.

Whatever the circumstances that beckon me to the craft room, these are the times when I ring the bell to say, "Stop, world. I'm getting off for a while." Then, as I work, I breathe in the fragrance of stress relief and escape from time and expectations to identify, categorize, and file thoughts and feelings. Another fragrance offers an invitation to embody joy—probably some days because I am feeling it and other days because I long for it. When I step back into the world, I am better equipped to deal with its challenges and, in the meantime, have learned or grown in some way.

I've shared these whispered messages of my quilts because, though my mind and heart may best define me as a space cadet, my earthbound feet walk life as a peasant seed planter. In the embracing of my own story and in taking in the shared stories of others, the common and differing threads become interwoven, embellishing my life, challenging my understanding of God, and equipping my vision to be able to experience God sightings even in the ordinary. Hopefully, this book has planted seeds that offer you a trip of your own to places where you have heard some whispered secrets just for you.